STAND UP PUT DOWNS

TRANSWORLD PUBLISHERS
61–63 Uxbridge Road, London W5 5SA
A Random House Group Company
www.transworldbooks.co.uk

First published in Great Britain
in 2011 by Bantam Press
an imprint of Transworld Publishers

A CIP catalogue record for this book
is available from the British Library.

ISBN 9780593068069

Addresses for Random House Group Ltd companies outside the UK
can be found at: www.randomhouse.co.uk
The Random House Group Ltd Reg. No. 954009

Typeset in Sefira
Printed and bound in Italy

2 4 6 8 10 9 7 5 3 1

STAND UP PUT DOWNS

THE BEST HECKLER PUT DOWNS FROM COMEDY'S MASTERS OF THE ART

Compèred by

RUFUS HOUND

BANTAM PRESS

LONDON · NEW YORK · TORONTO · SYDNEY · AUCKLAND

CONTENTS

Introduction

There are few traditions the West regards as noble, but killing people is one of them. Expect no medals for creeping up behind an old lady in a darkened alley, however. Oh no. Heroism is claimed only for smiting your enemy on the battlefield, the whites of the smitee's eyes visible to you, the smiter.

Whether it's the trenches, the boxing ring, the Thunderdome or the pavement in front of Yates's Wine Lodge, we celebrate those who emerge from skirmish with a smile on their face and blood on their scimitar. 'But what of this, Jester?', I hear you cry, your bejewelled goblet smashing atop your oaken feasting table. Well, friend, that is what this book is. A collection of epithets garnered from the theatre of war. A catalogue of weapons used to defend, parry, attack and destroy.

This is a museum of machetes.

If your experience of stand-up comedy has been restricted to that which your home can deliver via TV / internet / DVD / Space Laser / whatever, then my commiserations to you. You are a virgin. Stand-up on telly is like sex on telly. Pleasurable enough, but more enjoyable if you're actually there. Anyone who's watched the shiny American porn that dominates the world of carnal cinema understands that the pneumatic action onscreen is the result of planning, fabrication and editing. I'm sure that when Barbara took on those eleven dudes, her hair got pulled, her legs gave way, Barry went off too soon, etc. so what is shown has to be the edited highlights. Yes, you can see most of what happened, but you can't feel what it was like to actually be there. There's too much missing – the smells, the feel of things, how the air tasted … you're missing the deeply human bit.

We humans are an odd bunch. We started as tiny specks, then bigger specks, then we became little thingamajigs, then fish, then monkeys, then possibly sea-monkeys, then monkeys again before finally someone invented trousers and the human race was born. Over the course of two billion years it has been hardwired into us to fight, run, eat, screw and jostle to be head of the pack.

The same primeval instinct that makes gorillas beat their chests or stags lock antlers is the exact same instinct that makes some drunken twat in the back row shout at the comedian on stage. It's the moment that the young lion decides to kill the old lion and lead the pack himself. It's a power play. It is revolt.

Now, as any pirate worth their salt will tell you, at the first murmurings of mutiny, the captain must keelhaul the ringleader as an example to the others, or all too soon their grip on power will be too loose to keep hold, and they will be overthrown.

A comedian's time on stage is their tenure at the ship's wheel. Whether the Good Ship Comedy successfully docks in Port Hilarity or smashes into the rocks at Cape Refund is dependent on the navigational skills of the one steering. It is not a democracy. It's a dictatorship. As long as the crew/audience follows their orders to the letter ('Look at me! Listen! Laugh now!') no one need die, but the first audible rumblings of dissatisfaction tell the experienced Captain to ready the gangplank or else prepare for their own watery grave.

Alas, physical violence is frowned upon in the world of comedy, and thus gobby insurgents must be wounded psychologically. However, with limited time and limited information, the comedian can't afford to draw up a complete mental profile of their assailant. Thus, the tools of the trade are not those of precision but of blunt- force trauma.

There are things *no one* wants to hear about themselves. That they are sexually undesirable, mentally insufficient, their parents were awful, their job could only be performed by a moron, their friends only pretend to like them … these are the cyanide whispers that gently echo in the shadowy corridors of universal self-doubt. It is their universality that gives them power. Being publicly told any of these things has to not only embarrass the target, but also inspire a sense of 'I'm-so-glad-that-wasn't-me' in the rest of the crowd.

And even these 'universals' aren't quite universal. In many rooms across the country, the merest insinuation that the bellowing Stellafiend is in fact a homosexual is enough to earn his silence, but try that at Brighton's 'Bent Double' comedy night, and you will instead earn him a round of applause and possibly even a blowjob. Which is obviously not the idea.

So, 'heckler put-downs'. Unsurprisngly, there are a clutch of old favourites, tried and tested and still in regular use. There are those that really only work because of the person saying them. Then there are those borne of pure *inspirado*, when the planets aligned and the comedy gods smiled beatifically down. There's plenty of each amidst these pages, and absolutely every effort has been made to track down their creators and credit them accordingly. However, it appears that many of them are like Silvio Berlusconi's chlamydia – they must have come from someone, but god knows who. To these unknown soldiers, a debt of gratitude is owed. Thank you, whoever you are.

What might be confusing is why comedians need such a varied roster of verbal barbs. Well, stand-up comedy is like a porcelain battleship: for all its bullet-proof appearance, it's actually rather fragile. The wrong lighting, bad sound or poor room layout will break a night of comedy regardless of who's on the bill. Yet these insentient things are easy enough to put right; the people attending your gig, far less so. Yes, not everyone who shouts something from the darkness is trying to steal the show, they are not 'hecklers' per se, but funny people adding to the crowd's enjoyment. If the audience are laughing at the brilliance of this unexpected addition, the comedian should be big enough to commend the scamp for their joke, or top it, thus reassuring everyone that the funniest person in the room is on the stage and not in the third row. These are not the people I'm talking about (although I am including some tales about them in these pages). I'm talking about hecklers, of which there are really only four kinds:

1 The Attention Seeker

They think joining in is 'all part of the fun'. They'll be dicks throughout the entire set but rush up to the act in the interval with the offer of a drink and say, 'I was just helping you out, giving you something to work with!' Surprisingly, these are the people the stock put-downs normally work well on, as they're just after some attention. I sometimes feel bad for these guys, as berating someone for needing to be acknowledged when I'm standing on a stage, holding a microphone with lights pointing at me feels a bit hypocritical. But – as my old Nanna used to say – fuck 'em. Normally, once the Attention Seekers have had a bit of the spotlight, they'll shut up. They are embarrassable, and therefore controllable.

2 The Party

The party believe that this is their night. That their boss/stag/hen should be the centre of attention, that they are all on the single most important quest in the known universe and the last indignity they should be made to suffer is to sit there, silent, forced to listen to someone else banging on. They think they are free to gather each other's drinks requests, to share in-jokes and stories, cackling uproariously at one another, regardless of what the other 280 paying punters in the room might enjoy. What they don't realize, because they are drunk and therefore stupid (or maybe even just stupid), is that they are ruining it. Comedy is as much about the silences between the jokes as it is about the punchlines, and if those silences are broken by stilettoed harpies, twatty stags, shitty office parties or any other team formation of arseholes, then so are the jokes. Often, the smarter the comic on stage, the more vicious they are dealing with hecklers, as invariably they have considered every word and every pause, crafting their material so that it might build to an auspicious climax. If some idiot starts shouting random shit at them halfway through, it is ruined. For a musical act or a one-liner merchant, this is frustrating, but not the end of the world. If, on the other hand, an unwanted interjection comes at the denouement of a twenty-minute-long set-up, it can be utterly heartbreaking, and the punishment meted out from the stage will be flushed with the desperate, white-hot anger of a cornered viper.

3 The Offended

They have heard a joke that is not to their taste, and are now determined that the one who told it must fall. A comedian's success in this situation will depend entirely on whether or not the rest of the crowd found the joke offensive too. If they didn't, then the Offended is a tiny minority and playground rules apply – they're going down. They normally end up leaving, as the rest of the audience tell them to 'Shut up and fuck off'. If, however, the Offended represent the majority view, calling *them* an idiot is tantamount to calling most of the audience idiots too, in which case either apologize, or accept that you're about to crash and burn. Sadly, the law of the playground applies to *everyone* in the playground.

4 The Assassin

This is the worst kind, yet also the rarest. These are the hecklers who, against all odds, win. Not by a boorish war of attrition, but by a single killer line, funnier than the comedian's. The Assassin can only conquer if the act is already dying but, if they are, this is the equivalent of running them through to make sure they're dead.

Comedian, struggling at a gig on the Isle of Wight: 'I can't swim …'

Assassin: 'Well, fuck off now then, or you'll miss the ferry.'

Audience: 'Hahahahaha – yes. Do fuck off now.'

Comedian: [thinks] I must never do stand-up comedy again.

So there we are. Heckling and Hecklers. What now follow are some of the best put-downs wielded by the mightiest stand-up warriors of our time. I hope you enjoy them. Oh, and if, on these pages, you recognize yourself as the heckler and feel a small swell of pride – don't. Everyone thought you were a dick when it happened and everyone thinks you're a dick now.

Is That Your   1
Real Face?

The most obvious place for the comedian to start their counterattack is with their assailant's appearance. The comedian has to begin their heckler's verbal crucifixion in – at most – two seconds, so if they're fat, bald, ugly, poorly dressed (or the comedian thinks they can get away with insinuating that any of these things are true), then that's more than likely the first port of call.

However, if the comedian themself is poorly attired, attempting to mock the heckler for *their* sartorial shortcomings may backfire. Equally, if the turn is no oil painting, it's probably best to concentrate on one of the heckler's other physical failings – or grow a truly excellent moustache.

There's something brilliantly childish about insulting someone's looks to their face. Most people stop saying 'You're ugly and you smell' once they grow out of short trousers, so the audience's vicarious revisitation of this form of abuse is a deeply guilty pleasure. After all, asking an aggressor 'Is that your face or did your neck just throw up?' would normally be followed by a punch in the face, but in the confines of a comedy club, the knockout blow is merely verbal.

'If my dog had a face like yours I'd shave its arse and teach it to walk backwards.'
Anon

'Madam, you look like a Page 3 model. Admittedly, it's page 3 of the book of ugly, fat women.'
Gary Delaney

'I've seen you before, haven't I? Oh yes, I remember – I shit you earlier … and you wouldn't flush away.'
Arthur Smith

Heckler: 'You slept with my mate!'
Stephen Grant: 'I can't have – you don't look like you have a mate.'

'Now, now, manners cost nothing. Like that suit.'
Rufus Hound

'Ssshh, madam. Pay attention and you'll realize we have a lot in common, not just the beard.'
Markus Birdman

Heckler:
'I've fucked you; you were SHIT!'
Meryl O'Rourke:
'Yes, I remember, I was quite stiff, wasn't I? Trying to hold back the tidal wave of vomit.'

André Vincent to an overweight **female heckler**:
'Have a great time, madam, push the boat out – you've got the arms for it.'

Hi-tech Put-down
Meryl O'Rourke

❝ I was MCing at Cold Comedy in Milton Keynes and the evening was being interrupted by Ciall – a pubescent, geeky chatterbox with a girlfriend who exhibited the haunted gaze of someone in a hostage situation.

He had come with the sole intention of joining in, and was therefore near impossible to shut up.

During the interval our promoter mentioned that Ciall blogged about comedy, so I googled him on my phone and found a beautifully crap 'Things To Do Before I Die' list.

Marching on stage, iPhone in hand, I read out what I had found. Ciall went pale and the next ten minutes wrote itself thanks to entries such as 'Play Cluedo', 'Climb A Tree', 'Lose My Virginity' and 'Sleep With A Woman From Every Country In The World' (considering that his girlfriend hadn't even taken off her coat, I presumed the last two were not going to be crossed off any time soon).

I hope this story had a happy ending in that Ciall not only discovered the joys of Cluedo, but learned never to interrupt a comic – and that his girlfriend copped off with someone who doesn't see her as simply something to tick off a 'to do' list.

The future is here, and it's part of our artillery.

'Is that your real face or are you still celebrating Halloween?'
Arthur Smith

Female heckler: 'You've got a small cock.'
Toby Hadoke: 'When something's been in a mouth as big as yours, it's bound to seem small in comparison.'

Heckler: 'What's up with your hair?!'
Milton Jones: 'Stay calm, everyone, let me handle this. I get paid to look stupid … do you?'

Heckler: 'You're a slag!'

Meryl O'Rourke: 'You're right about that, sir. I've had sex with everyone in this room, apart from you … I wonder why that would be?'

Female heckler: 'That is an ugly shirt.'

Rufus Hound: 'Sister, unless you're the mayoress or the world's shittest Mr T impersonator, I'd lose some of that cheap gold jewellery before you criticize how people look.'

'I thought I told you to stay in the car and bark at strangers, you ugly cunt!'

Roy Chubby Brown

Heckler: 'I met you when I was at medical school.'

Frank Skinner: 'Ah yes, you were the one in the jar.'

Craig Campbell to a **female heckler**: 'Do you think just because you're a lady you're immune from me mocking you? [To the **lighting guy**] Can you turn the lights up on stage, so I don't have to see this monster's hideous face?'

'I'm sorry, I don't speak Orc.'
Brendan Dodds

If You Prefer a Milder Heckler . . .

Brendan Dodds

66 There are some heckles you can never recover from. While gigging as part of a four-man sketch team, we found ourselves at Just The Tonic in Nottingham. It was a bank holiday weekend, and the 200-plus punters were rowdy and more drunk than usual. The acts before us did punchy, aggressive jokes, getting to the laugh as quickly as possible.

It was a tough crowd for frivolous sketch-comedy and our quick-fire opener was met with blank stares from the bemused audience. 'You're not funny' came quickly, and we acknowledged the heckle, but without raising much of a laugh. Our first character arrived – a minstrel in a floppy green hat, who sings all his lines in medieval ballads. 'Who's this guy?' we asked, by way of introduction. Before the minstrel could begin, a man in the centre of the audience rose to his feet (never a good sign). 'It's one of you guys in a fucking hat, and you're still not fucking funny.'

As we switched cardboard props backstage, the headliner, legendary comedian Stewart Lee, leaned in and offered kind words of encouragement: 'Don't worry, mate, everyone has bad gigs.' Unfortunately he spoke directly into my colleague's live radio mic, which dutifully projected his words to the crowd. Heckles from the audience are tough, but it's something else altogether when they come from one of the most well-respected stand-ups in the land. **99**

Heckler: 'You're ugly.'
Jim Smallman: 'And yet your missus still prefers me to you.'

Comedian to a bald **heckler**: 'Is that your head or has your neck blown a bubble?' **Anon** (courtesy of **Peter Rosengard**)

Adam Bloom to a **female heckler**: 'I actually saw you at the bar before the show and, I shouldn't say this, but I got a semi hard-on… Yeah, because I had a full hard-on at the time.'

Heckler: 'I'm the Pope!'
Meryl O'Rourke: 'And it looks like you've been kissing the tarmac with some force there.'

Lucy Porter during a routine about dating a ventriloquist: 'One of the weirdest things is when you start hearing voices when a guy's going down on you.'
Heckler: 'It was probably just the echo.'

Toby Hadoke

to a **woman** who interrupted him just before a punchline: 'See, you put me off my rhythm there, much like what would happen to a fella who's making mad, passionate love to you and suddenly, by accident, catches sight of your face.'

'When god put teeth in your mouth he ruined a perfectly good arsehole.' **Anon**

'Try not to draw too much attention to yourself – your girlfriend might finally notice who she's with.' **Brendan Dodds**

The Self-Knowledge Impregnator
Simon Munnery

❝ **Long long ago there was a futuristic cabaret show called Cluub Zarathustra, whose cast included Stewart Lee, Kevin Eldon, Roger Mann, Sally Phillips, Richard 'Tom Miles' Thomas, opera singer Loré Lixenberg and various other bit-part players and contributors. It was hosted by a superhuman übercompère calling himself 'The League Against Tedium' (myself).**

There was a procedure for dealing with hecklers. If anyone heckled, the League would exclaim, 'Activate the Self-Knowledge Impregnator'. Sirens would wail, darkness would fall, and a team of six would carry a large black box right up to the miscreant. The League would then ask the heckler if he was aware of what he was, and before he had time to answer, fire the device, which consisted of a powerful mains camera flash at the back, with the word 'CUNT' cut out of a large wooden plate at the front, covered with a thin layer of gauze to maintain the surprise. The League would then say, 'What about now?' as the heckler tried to blink away the word that was now burned into his retinas. **❞**

Show Me Your
Brain Cell

2

A heckler looks at the act on stage, sees how in control of the room they are, how everyone facing them seems to laugh on cue, how they have a microphone (so are therefore louder than anyone else in the room by far), how well lit and visible they are ... the heckler looks at all of that and thinks, 'I can take him/her'. This is because the heckler is a moron.

I mean, you'd have to be, right? To realize what an unfair fight it is, and yet still decide you fancy it? As such, it's a pretty good bet that the lone voice in the darkness is not that of the Mensa president. 'But the put-down must be easy then, right? Like shooting mackerel in a matchbox!' I hear you cry. Well, yes ... and no. If your heckler is of only subnormal intelligence, then one stinging rebuke is all it should take to win their silence. If, however, you're dealing with a proper fuckwit, they won't have the wherewithal to realize they've been bested. Inevitably, it will end up with security escorting them from the building whilst the rest of the room applaud. An ignoble exit.

'Some comedians have plants in the audience. I get a fucking vegetable.' **Anon**

'Were you born this stupid or did someone punch you in the elbow when you were picking your nose?' **Rufus Hound**

'You've got to excuse that guy. I saw him sipping water in the gents' loo earlier … the toilet seat came down and hit him in the back of the neck.' **Anon** (courtesy of **Peter Rosengard**)

'Three hundred million sperm and you were the fastest. What would the slowest be like? Presumably not that different.' **Henning Wehn**

'It's important to have a scale of heckles, so that we all know where we stand. The one you just did? Let's say that that one … is zero.' **Stuart Goldsmith**

Heckler: 'You fat twat.'
Roy Chubby Brown: 'Did you watch *Playschool* as a lad?'
Heckler: 'Yes.'
Roy Chubby Brown: 'Which fucking window do you want to go through?'

Chris Stokes: 'It's nice to see so many of you here, especially as it means you're all missing *My Big Fat Gypsy Wedding*...'
Heckler: 'Sky Plus, mate!'
Chris Stokes: 'Is that so you don't miss your star turn on it?'

'When someone tells you to fuck off, do you get a sense of déjà vu?'
Sean Meo

Ed Byrne (after getting heckled): 'Look, when I pause, it's called "comic timing", it's not "cue the fuckwit" … so imagine … [gets heckled again]. Pardon me? What? See, this is the difference between saying funny things and just saying things. That's why I've got a microphone and you haven't. The only time you get a microphone is when they put you on the drive-thru counter. So, as I was saying [heckled again] … oh, here we go, he's just not giving up, is he? "I'm fucking determined, I don't care! I'm going to say things and still no fucker is going to laugh but I'm going to go home feeling very good about myself!" Which is the difference between you and everybody else here. You see, you're going to go home tonight and the next day you're going to talk to all your mates … all right, your one mate, you're gonna say, "Dad… I was really funny last night, you'll be really proud of me. I went *wooooha* and everybody thought I was brilliant…" And everybody else is going to go home and say, "The comedy was brilliant, but there was one fucking cockhead that just wouldn't shut the fuck up!"'

'One day soon we're going to need a minimum of one A-Level even to buy a pound of potatoes – and you're going to starve.'

Arnold Brown

'If you could raise your intelligence just a couple of notches you could be a plant.'
Anon (courtesy of **Peter Rosengard**)

'If you are going to heckle, try to wait for a gap when I'm not talking so people can hear what you're saying.'
Richard Herring

'Sorry, I can't understand what you're saying – I'm wearing a moron filter.'
Arthur Smith

'Glad you came. Shame your dad did.'
Joe Heenan

Voice from the upper stalls: 'Yeh baldy bollox.'
Brendan O'Carroll: 'Who said that?'
Voice: 'I did.'
Brendan O'Carroll: 'Well, you're right! ...
But I'm the baldy bollox with your 25 euros in me pocket.'

'Look at this guy, the only person to ever be turned down for a Matalan membership because he failed the IQ test.' [Pretends to work for Matalan.] 'Just sign here.' [Then mimes a man scrawling everywhere except where the pretend Matalan employee just indicated.]

Rufus Hound

Heckler: 'BNP! BNP! BNP!'
Chris Stokes: 'You are everything that is wrong with humanity, you sorry flap of infected vagina.'

'Well, at least now we all know who writes the comments on YouTube.'
Gary Delaney

Hal Cruttenden to a young **female heckler**: 'That's fine, you're very young and very pretty, but one day your looks will fade and you'll have to rely on your personality and you'll be screwed.'

Linda and the Rugby Crowd

Warren Lakin

❝ I am the partner of the late Linda Smith, and was responsible for compiling and editing the book *I Think the Nurses Are Stealing My Clothes: The Very Best of Linda Smith.*

In her earlier years as a comedy club stand-up, Linda would often include a whole segment in her act about the world of sport – as far as I know, at the time she was the only female comic who did that.

Linda was an enthusiastic follower of cricket and football – West Ham United was her team. But she had a healthy disregard for golf and rugby in particular. The rugby stuff originated from her time at the University of Sheffield. Her experiences of the rowdy and disruptive male rugby crowd gave rise to classic jibes such as 'Rugby – a game for men with no fear of head injuries … and with no reason to fear them!' The other one she regularly employed on stage was aimed at rowdy and hapless groups of male hecklers – rugby clubs included. In response to their inevitable calls of 'Get your tits out,' Linda would retort, 'Why – is it time for your feed?' ❞

'You might heckle me now but when I get home I've got a chicken in the oven.'
Harry Hill

'How about you come back with your remaining chromosomes and heckle me again?'
Russell Kane

'Look, it's all right to donate your brain to science but shouldn't you have waited till you died?'
Arthur Smith

'You're like a dog that's been spayed – you just don't get it.'
André Vincent

'Why don't you go into that corner and finish evolving?'
Russell Kane

Heckler to **John Hegley**: 'Show us your cock.'
John Hegley: 'I will if you show me your brain cell.'
Heckler: 'At least it'll be bigger than your cock.'

Heckler: 'I don't come here to think.'
Bill Hicks: 'Well, tell me where you do go and I'll meet you there.'

'Poor chap, he has delusions of adequacy.'
Arthur Smith

To Heckle or Not to Heckle?
André Vincent

The Edinburgh Fringe 1992. It all started at the Gilded Balloon's infamous *Late'n' Live*, an after-hours drinking den and comedy cabaret show. The audience is mostly made up of young festival performers full of vim and dreams, and older acts still supping from their vessel of bitter.

This particular night, a comedian – who it was escapes me – was being lamely heckled. 'You're not funny … tell us a joke!' was as good as it got. What affronted me was not the low level of the jibes, but that they were coming from actors. I was shocked that they could enjoy ruining the night for everyone. So I decided to ask a few questions to find out who they were and where their show was.

The next afternoon, I went to the Southside Theatre where the hecklers' play was on. After about fifteen minutes I started up with, 'You're not funny … tell us a joke!' I was soon bored by my own barrage and left long before the interval. News of my exploits raced around the festival – the gossip was all about 'revenge heckling' and how the next hit would be on a comic.

I have to say I was pretty proud of my actions, and one of the Southside stage managers, who also worked at the Balloon, congratulated me that night on my exploits. As my ego flamed, she then told me that the play being performed by the band of disruptive actors was actually the one *after* the one I had heckled. Oops…

The Irish Have a
Word for
People Like You

… and that word is 'gobshite'. According to the Internet (an unquestionably accurate source), it stems from the conjunction of the words 'gob' and 'shite' and means 'One who has an endless torrent of shit pouring out of the hole in their face'.

It's a specific word, for a specific type of person. When I temped for big companies – before I was a comedian – I learned that every office in the world is allocated at least one. You know, the sort of person who enthusiastically opens their mouth in meetings, instantly causing everyone else to roll their eyes and beg God to end the pointless noise. This person has never said anything of value or use in their whole life, and today is but another day in which that fact is unlikely to change.

Yes, 'gobshite' eloquently describes those people who just won't shut up, despite having nothing to say. Certain of their own brilliance, these people swagger noisily and late into the comedy club and shout bizarre, random things in the mistaken belief that the performer onstage could receive no finer gift than their company. On some level, all hecklers are gobshites, but this chapter has been set aside for the gobshitiest.

'You're not funny, and no one likes you. Don't you remember that from school?'
Anon

'Do I hear the long-term side effects of Junior Aspirin?'
Arnold Brown

Heckler: 'Shut yer mouth and give yer brain a chance.'
John Cooper Clarke: 'I can't hear yer, mate, yer mouth's full o'shit!'

Chris Stokes to somebody generally being a disruptive pain: 'I've got your number – it's seven hundred and dickhead.'

Craig Campbell to a **heckler** calling the shots: 'Hey, man. Why don't you try to remember some place you have influence and go there.'

'Your heckle is in a queue and will be dealt with whenever I can be arsed to deal with it.'
Anon

Mitch Benn to a **heckler** behaving childishly: 'Look, have a cereal bar and put *Peppa Pig* on. Daddy's talking to the grown-ups.'

Sean Meo to a mouthy **female heckler**: 'I'm beginning to think you're the reason blowjobs were invented.'

'All men are pigs, especially you, sir. Unfortunately, I can't eat pork.'
Shazia Mirza

Heckler: 'The sleeves on your jacket are slightly frayed.'
Richard Herring: 'Yes, you're right, they are.'

Relentless **heckler** (at a gig in a deconsecrated church): 'I'm just an empty soul!'
Steve Williams: 'No, you're a total arse soul!'

Keeping an Eye Out
Steve Williams

" I was performing in the North-East to raise money for *Children in Need*. It was a really great night apart from one table of idiots down at the front who talked over all the comedians.

When the compère announced me on, before I even got to the mic, Sir Talk-a-Lot and the Knights of the Loud Table turned their chairs away from the stage and started chatting louder then ever. Distracted and slightly annoyed, I asked the ringleader if everything was OK and suggested he turn to face the front. He shouted back that he didn't want to because he only had one eye. Sensing he was lying, I pointed out that Pudsey Bear only had one eye and he was facing the front. To which Sir Talk-a-Lot responded by scooping out his artificial eye and lobbing it at me on stage.

Tom Jones gets sexy ladies chucking underwear at him; I get some nutter throwing his eye at me. I'd never been heckled optically before so, slightly shocked, under pressure and definitely not wanting to be outdone, I popped his eye in my mouth, turned to the audience and said, 'Good evening, I'm Stevie Williams – that's Stevie Williams with three I's.' "

'Could someone please put something in her mouth before I do. Because I need a shit.'
Rufus Hound

'Haven't you noticed that when I speak, people laugh, and when you speak, people go silent and lose the will to live? That's why, in a minute, everyone is going to cheer … carry me shoulder-high around the room … and dump me, arse first, on your head, so you'll have to wear me like a Human Centipede.'
Steve Shanyaski

Boothby Graffoe: 'Have you enjoyed yourselves?'
Heckler: 'No!'
Boothby Graffoe: 'Ah, madam, that's because you're labouring under a lot of unnecessary guilt. When you were a small child, the reason your father spent so much of his time with his cock in your mouth was to shut you up; it wasn't a sexual thing. So relax.'

'Don't be surprised if you hear footsteps behind you on the way home … that's your soul trying to get away from your personality.'
Markus Birdman

'I bet your girlfriend wishes your dick was as big as your mouth.' **Anon**

'Little tip, next time someone offers you a penny for your thoughts, sell.'
Adam Bloom

Jim Jefferies to an abusive **female heckler**: 'Darling, I could never make love to you, I could only ever fuck you. And I wouldn't even want to do that as once I've come on your face it will take most of the fake tan off!'

'You're like a broken radio which, however much you tune it, only picks up arsehole.'
Brendan Dodds

Gonged off at the Comedy Store

Arnold Brown

> I made my debut in stand-up comedy on the opening night of the Comedy Store at the Gargoyle Club in Soho in May 1979, the beginnings of the Alternative Comedy movement in the UK. It was a conscious antidote to the racist and sexist attitudes of Bernard Manning, Jim Davidson et al and its seismic rumbles changed live comedy overnight.

A few years later *The Young Ones* exploded onto our TV screens, featuring many of the luminaries who began at the Comedy Store, namely Alexei Sayle (the resident compère), Rik Mayall, Ade Edmondson, Nigel Planer, Peter Richardson, Keith Allen, Dawn French and Jennifer Saunders. Ah yes, and there was also Ben Elton.

The opening night was exciting and the punters were plied with free champagne. To add to the atmosphere of mayhem there was the infamous gong by which the audience could egg on the compère to get rid of any performer they didn't like.

My debut was somewhat less than successful. It was my very first appearance on stage. In fact, I was so ingenuous I didn't realize you had to have prepared material... I thought you just made it up as you went along.

However, I did have one 'joke' in my head. 'Good evening, my name is Arnold Brown and I am an accountant. I check things...' and was about to add, 'Can you hear me at the back?' when someone shouted out, 'We can't hear you at the back!' Alexei obliged the audience and I was gonged off... But I did come back the next night – despite public demand!

Heckler: 'Fuck off, you fat cow!'
Jo Brand: 'I deliberately keep my weight up so that a tosser like you won't fancy me.'

'Listen, I get it. The last time you were in a room with a man holding a microphone you were on *The Jeremy Kyle Show*, but trust me, small fry, now is not your time to join in.'
Rufus Hound

Sean Meo to a persistent **heckler**: 'Just keep still, mate, we're waiting for the sniper to get a clear shot.'

Female heckler: 'Suck the blood from my bleeding cunt, you motherfucker!'
Tiernan Douieb: 'I've never heard such an abusive heckle.'
Omid Djalili (in the crowd): *'I've* never heard such an abusive heckle.'
Tiernan Douieb: 'And that's coming from a man who's been described as "The Brown Danny DeVito".'

'Sir, a good audience is like good cuisine. It takes just one dick in it to spoil it.'
Alexis Dubus (as Marcel Lucont)

Heckler (at the end of Rufus's set, during a show in mid-December): 'You're shit!'
Rufus Hound: 'Well, fella, the way I like to look at it is this. There will be people in the audience tonight who get what I do and like it. They probably get it and like it because they're a bit like me. They share my worldview, my hopes and dreams, my sense of humour. I really like those guys. However, there are also people who aren't like me, who won't get it and don't like it and, well, I hope those people get cancer. Merry Christmas.'

Henning Wehn to a particularly loud **heckler**:
'Where did you learn to whisper? In a Panzer?'

'Your bus leaves in ten minutes…
Be under it.' **John Cooper Clarke**

Bill Hicks to a **heckler** who persists in calling out random words and names throughout his set, culminating with 'Jimmy Shorts': '"Jimmy Shorts"? He's not here. He's not gonna be here, now what? Now where are we? We're here with you interrupting me again, you fucking idiot! That's where we're fuckin' at! Once again, the useless wastes of fucking flesh that have ruined everything good in the goddamn world! That's where we're at! Hitler had the right idea, he was just an underachiever! Kill them all, Adolf, all of 'em! Jew, Mexican, American, white, kill them all! Start over! The experiment didn't work! Rain forty days, please fucking rain to wash these fucking turds out of my fucking life! Wash these human wastes of flesh and bone off this planet! I pray to you, God, kill these fucking people!'

'Well done, sir. You've just won a weekend for two, picking cockles in Morecambe Bay. Now fuck off.'
Danny James

Henning Wehn to the **audience** at a rough gig: 'This is worse than Nuremberg.'

'This is quite a big venue, I can't really get into one-to-ones. In a smaller room … I'd still ignore you, you cunt, now shut up!'
Ricky Gervais

Heckler: 'You're a lesbian.'
Rhona Cameron: 'Yes, I am indeed. There's a black comic on later … are you going to remind them that they're black?'

Talk to Your Heckler
Rhona Cameron

" When I first started out, in the early 1990s, I never really suffered from heckling. I was a lot tougher in those days and I gave off a 'I'm working class, gay and Scottish, don't fuck with me' vibe. After a few months I decided to introduce some lesbian material and as I was the first comic to do so, I think people just listened in fascination. I did a gag about people staring at me and my girlfriend on holiday which ended up talking about being drunk and fist-fucking on a beach. Audiences loved it.

As a comic I talk in monologues; I don't do soundbites. If I did ever get heckled, I had no quick, standard comeback, preferring to treat every cunt who felt the need to shout out as a unique individual case. The classic one that almost all comics got from some drone was 'You're not funny'. So I'd be like, 'What was that, sorry?' to which they would mutter something. 'Come on, say it so everyone can hear.' [Nothing.] 'You hear that sound at the end of my sentences that the crowd are making?' [Pause, whilst drunk members of audience catch up.] 'Well, that's laughter.' [Pause for applause.] 'So I think you will find that in this context, here this evening, I have in fact been funny.' [Bigger cheer and applause.] 'Anything else you would like to add?' [Silence.] 'Well, should you want to interrupt my set again with a pointless lot of shite, do feel free.'

There have been mad moments, though, in the very early days. On one occasion, at the Comedy Café in Old Street, London, I was off my head and totally lost it with a heckler. I removed my pants and put them in his pint. (I should add that I was wearing a dress.) "

'I bet as a child you were such a cunt that Michael Jackson made you sleep in your own fucking bed.'
Danny James

'Stop shouting stuff out. I'm sure you mean well but it always ends badly. I remember I did a gig where I hadn't even got to the microphone before a woman shouted, "Get your knob out!" Now, admittedly, it should never have been in her.'
Markus Birdman

Jim Jefferies: 'Nobody likes you! Want me to prove it? … Everyone put your hand up in the air. [Everyone raises their hand.] Everyone point at that man. [Everyone points at the man.] Everyone shout CUNT! [Everyone shouts CUNT!] Now, I got women to say that word! And women HATE that word… But not as much as they hate you!'

'I see we have a little joker in the pack. Just to remind you, sir, the joker is largely considered the most useless card in the pack, to be discarded so the game of cards can continue. Get out!'
Alexis Dubus (as Marcel Lucont)

Heckler: 'Tell us a joke.'
Jim Smallman: 'Up to and including this moment, your pointless little life.'

Heckler (after his disruptive mate has been dealt with by Rufus): 'Just carry on with the show!'
Rufus Hound: 'Oh, we can, can we? That's very good of you. Ladies and gentlemen, the mayor is here! The mayor is here and has decreed that we may continue with our little distraction here this evening. Thank you, your lordship, thank you!'

Nigel Planer (as Neil from *The Young Ones*): 'Oh no! I'm being heckled! Oh no! What do I do? Got to think of something witty and spontaneous to put them down! Heavee! I know, I'll use the witty and spontaneous put-down book! Hang on. Here it is. Erm… [gets out small book with "Witty and Spontaneous Put-downs" written on the cover, and turns pages quite slowly.] Erm… No, wait, there's a really good one in here somewhere. Erm… Oh, here's one, here's one – Fuck off! Oh no! I've used the best one first. Hang on, hang on… [turns more pages in a panic.] OK, here's one – in ten years' time, right? They're going to have, like, educationally streamed supermarkets, OK? … and you'll need, like, at least three GCSEs to buy a pound of sausages, yeah? … And you're going to starve.'

Arnold Brown (in response to a **mass heckle**): 'A bond has been established between myself, the performer, and you the audience … I think we can sum it up in one word – resentment.'

Bob Monkhouse: 'Madam, do you make that much noise when you're making love?'
Female heckler: 'No.'
Bob Monkhouse: 'Well, would someone please come and fuck her.'

Heckler: 'Get on with it!'
Jim Jefferies: 'You want more jokes? An Englishman, an Irishman and a Scotsman walk into a bar – and call you a cunt!'

'What a waste of a life.' **Arthur Smith**

Rufus Hound (looking to the **bar staff**): 'Can we get some crayons and a menu for this guy to colour in please?'

'You're the kind of girl who thinks "friends with benefits" means seeing someone who's claiming jobseeker's allowance.'
Brendan Dodds

'I know I seem really nice but if you carry on I'll follow you home, kill you and wear your skin.'
Hal Cruttenden

Henning Wehn to an aggressive **heckler**: 'What are you so angry about? Has the Marmite price gone up?'

'You're a big lad. Do you find you cry a lot?'
Meryl O'Rourke

Heckler: 'Oh my god, it's a fat Pete Doherty!'
Jim Smallman: 'Indeed it is. And before I got here I fucked the fat Kate Moss.'

Words for 4
the Wasted

By this stage in the book, you may be thinking, 'I didn't know there were so many arseholes in the world. Why would you buy a ticket to a comedy show just to sit there trying to ruin it?' It's a fine question, and one that thousands of comedians have asked – either aloud or internally – since time immemorial.

The truth is that very few punters take to their seats with sabotage in mind. Most, in my experience, have just been going through a bit of a tough time of late and have thought that a night in a comedy club may well be the perfect way to cheer themselves up. And then they start drinking. Yes, it is our old friend **Alcohol** that both embitters and emboldens, whispering directly to the heckler's Id:

'Your life is awful. *This* is awful, you should really say something.'

'But everyone will think we're a dick if we do that!' cries **Ego**.

'Shut up and have a drink,' replies **Alcohol**. 'Me and Id are about to become gods! Gods! And nothing anyone says will silence us!'

Poor old **Ego**. He tried. Alas, due to **Alcohol**, he failed.

'I remember when I had *my* first beer.'
Steve Martin

'The funny thing about alcohol is that it doesn't change who we are, it just makes us less inhibited, often revealing the person we really are. And bad news, dude. You're this guy. That's gotta really suck.'
Rufus Hound

Toby Hadoke (to a **bullish drunk**): 'Ah, I see the alcohol has given you a bravado that your wit and personality simply don't justify.'

'I thought alcoholics were supposed to be anonymous!'
Anon

The Second Coming
Steve Gribbin

Sometimes audience interaction can take on unpleasantly physical dimensions. I was playing a gig with my comedy partner Brian Mulligan at the 1989 Glastonbury Festival. It was mid-afternoon and there were about two thousand people in the tent. Some way into the gig a bloke got up and walked across the front of the stage. We couldn't help noticing that he looked remarkably like Jesus.

He was actually walking out of the tent on his way to another gig, but the opportunity proved too delicious to resist. Brian said to him: 'All right, Jesus … how's it going?' The man turned round to acknowledge the cheers of the crowd, but I couldn't help myself. I said: 'We've been waiting for you to reappear for the last two thousand years … what took you so long?'

Something within him seemed to snap, and he sprinted towards the stage screaming blue murder. He leapt up on to the stage, grabbed me by the throat and proceeded to strangle me. It being Glastonbury, there were no bouncers to come to my rescue, and I thought this might be it. I began to black out.

Luckily Brian hit him over the head with the guitar, which momentarily stunned him and allowed the stagehands to manhandle him off into the wings, still screaming. I think drugs may have been involved.

As I recovered, I looked at the crowd and just said: 'Jesus Christ!' to one of the biggest laughs of the whole weekend.

'If you're going to come and heckle, be prepared. Don't get so pissed you can't think. That's the first rule of heckling. Second rule of heckling: maybe bring your own amplification system.'
Richard Herring

'When everyone said they were coming out for a few pints tonight, they didn't mean "of petrol", cowboy.'
Rufus Hound

Brendon Burns to a drunk and persistent **female heckler**: 'Congratulations, love, you're now the star of my next ten wanks.'

Hands Up for a Heckle
Rob Rouse

" My worst memory of a gig would have to be one night, many years ago, in Luton. I'd not been doing stand-up for long and, as with most bad experiences in life, I can only remember shards of information; the rest has been erased in an act of self-preservation.

There were about three hundred people in the club and we were told beforehand that most of them worked at the nearby Vauxhall car plant and that huge job losses were expected in the next few weeks, so the crowd might not be in the best of spirits. I couldn't have felt like more of a child when I walked on to the stage, unbelievably wet behind the ears. They needed hard, gritty, grown up comedy, something substantial and meaningful; not the sort of surreal whimsy I was peddling at that stage of my career.

The audience tolerated my nervous attempts to entertain them for what felt like an eon. Eventually, though, any vaguely supportive attempts to laugh ebbed away into a silence so deafening I could hear my pulse beating in my ears. All moisture left my mouth and I desperately tried to cover the fact that my legs were disco-dancing beneath me to a nonexistent tune.

Eventually a woman in the middle of the room put her hand up. She put her hand up! Hollowed out, terrified and resigned to the reality of my situation, I weakly uttered, 'Yes?' To which she replied, 'Excuse me, but where is this going?' To this day, I genuinely can't remember whether I said anything in response, carried on, wet myself or just walked off. Whatever happened, my brain has chosen to forget it. Self-preservation. **"**

Battle of the Sexiest

If I'm arguing that heckling is simply the verbal expression of those same primitive instincts our forebears channelled as chest beating (and I am, by the way), then it will come as no surprise that the mating rights so prized by our monkey granddads are given equal prominence in any spoken battle for primacy.

In other words, no bloke likes being called a virgin, and no woman likes to be labelled a slut – at least not in public or without a premium-rate phone number being involved. Casting aspersions on the dynamism or profligacy of somebody's bedroom gymnastics not only embarrasses the target, but encourages the rest of the pack/audience to laugh hard at this assertion. After all, anyone who isn't laughing must be a sexual wash-out themselves, right? No one wants that thought of them, and so the laugh of the audience is one that's not only directed at the heckler, but at any doubts concerning their own sexual prowess.

Yup, if you want to make someone feel bad about themselves, hit them where it hurts – right in the underpants.

'You're confident, aren't you? So confident that you seem like the sort of woman who would Rohypnol her own drink.'
Russell Kane

Rosie Wilby: 'I haven't always been open about being gay…'
Male heckler: 'I love lesbians.'
Rosie Wilby: 'Good! Me too.'
Male heckler: 'Will you have a threesome with me and my girlfriend?'
Rosie Wilby: 'Of course … but it'll be you that gets left out.'

Markus Birdman to a **male heckler**: 'I didn't hear what you said, but it sounded a bit like "I like men".'

'You should have an agent, mate. Why sit in the dark handling yourself?'
Anon

'Aww. And it sounded so good when you were practising in front of the mirror, masturbating.'
Brendan Dodds

'Where's your girlfriend? Outside grazing, I presume.'
Jo Brand

Fifty-something, overweight **male heckler**: 'You're shit!'
Joe Lycett: 'Are you flirting with me? [No response from heckler] … because I'd rather fist myself.'

Abnormal
Joe Lycett

" I do material about being bisexual as it's something people have presumptions about that can be punctured and manipulated for comic effect. At one gig, after mentioning my sexuality, a man in his seventies recoiled from me as I approached him. I asked him why he was so scared of me, to which he replied, 'Because I'm normal.' That word is something that has always irritated me as it's so dismissive of so many people. I asked him what he meant by this, specifically if he thought a white, heterosexual male was 'normal'. 'That'll do it,' he replied.

I'd never come up against such backward thinking in such a direct way and part of me felt like I should explain to him that his views were damaging and ill informed. Instead, the heat of the moment took over and I shouted, 'This calls for a game of GAY CHICKEN' (a game played by confused schoolboys where they 'pretend' to be gay, but essentially just touch each other's thighs). I obviously didn't play gay chicken with him, that's sexual assault. I just flirted as I explained the rules, but I like to think it was potentially more powerful to gently plant the idea of my ball-sack being in his mouth. **"**

Steph Davies: 'I'm actually celebrating tonight because I've now been single for two years.'
Heckler: 'I'll do you, luv.'
Steph Davies: 'Which school of chat-up lines did you go to, because to be perfectly honest I'd ask for your money back. Thanks for the offer but I'm going to be busy washing my hair for the next … ten years.'
Heckler: 'You know you want it.'
Steph Davies: 'Two million sperm and *you* got through … fucking hell!'

Heckler: 'Tell us a joke.'
Danielle Ward (pointing to heckler's girlfriend): She thinks you're good in bed.'

'If cocks had wings your mouth would have landing lights.'
Julia Morris

'Hey, buddy, you oughta save your breath. You'll need it later to blow up your inflatable date.'
Rodney Dangerfield

Mike Gunn: 'Hello, my name is Michael and I have a sister called Wendy.'
Heckler: 'I know her.'
Mike Gunn: 'Really?'
Heckler: 'Yes, I've shagged her.'
Mike Gunn: 'Well, I'd keep quiet about it if I were you; she's only seven.'

Heckler: 'You suck.'
Richard Pryor: 'My dick.'

Adam Hills: 'Is anyone celebrating anything tonight?'
Male audience member: 'Yeah, my first blowjob.'
Adam Hills: 'And now you're drinking to try and get the taste out of your mouth.'

Heckler: 'You're rubbish!'
Danielle Ward: 'You're lonely.'

Dumb Waiter
Mike Gunn

❝ I was booked to perform for two hundred conservative, elderly accountants at a swanky hotel in London. Not an ideal demographic as I was dressed as an undertaker, telling jokes about death.

The huge room was crowded with tables and it took me ten minutes to work my way through the audience. I had to ask people to move their chairs in to reach the stage.

After fifteen minutes I hadn't received a single laugh and the audience was staring with undisguised animosity. As the inevitable heckling started I said goodnight but couldn't face picking through the tables again so I ducked through a door to the side of the stage and found myself in the hotel kitchens.

There was a cleaner sitting there who told me the only way out was back into the room from which I had just fled. Then I spotted the dumb waiter – a small pulley-operated shelf that was used to lower plates into the room below. Desperate, I convinced the cleaner to help me use it. I squeezed myself into the space and he began to lower me down. With a bump I hit the bottom, pushed the doors open and peered out. To my horror I found myself staring at the ageing accountants. Whilst I had been planning my escape from the kitchens, they had changed rooms and were now dancing in the ballroom below. With as much dignity as I could muster, I extracted myself from the platform and walked out, the crowd parting with silent contempt. ❞

Ray Peacock to a **female heckler**: 'I've absolutely no interest in fucking you.'
Female heckler: 'In your dreams…'
Ray Peacock: 'In my dreams? I'd have to eat a lot of cheese.'

Heckler: 'Fuck off, you're not funny.'
Jim Smallman to woman with **heckler**: 'How long have you known this guy?'
Woman: 'It's our first date.'
Jim Smallman: 'Is it going well?'
Woman: 'No.'
Jim Smallman: 'Tell you what, here's my phone number for later on. I'll treat you better. 07872…'
Heckler: 'Fuck off, that's bang out of order!'
Jim Smallman: 'To be honest, mate, I don't really fancy her. But I would fuck her just to annoy you.'

Johnny Cochrane: 'I've noticed two rules about hecklers I come across. One is that they say "have" when they mean to say "am" and the second is that they always have small cocks.'
Heckler: 'That's not true! I've been told that I HAVE a massive cock!'

Heckler: 'Get your tits out!'
Catie Wilkins (pauses and squints into audience): 'Uncle Joe?'

Heckler: 'You're going grey, mate.'
Markus Birdman: 'What's wrong with grey hair?'
Heckler: 'Paedophiles have grey hair!'
Markus Birdman: 'Was your uncle grey?'

'Nigel, it's over, can't you understand that?'
Jeremy Hardy

André Vincent to blonde **female heckler**: 'It's been scientifically proven that blondes have more fun.'
Heckler cheers.
André Vincent: 'Did I say fun? Sorry, I meant venereal disease.'

Keep it in 6
the Family

When comedians run out of targets based on their foes'
inadequacies, it's time to move on to their nearest and dearest.
As you will see, spouses, siblings, uncles, dads are all fair
game. However, if you want to really get under their skin it's
time to bust an oral cap in the ass of the heckler's mummy.

After all, your mother grew you in herself. Unless you're a mother,
you have no idea how much this is the physiological equivalent of
being turned inside out. Pregnancy and birth bring with them a
selflessness that borders on the miraculous. In short, your mother is
a saint – a living fucking saint.

Anyone suggesting anything to the contrary is striking not merely
against you, but against the notion of all that's good in the world.
So, if you're trading insults, chances are that it won't be long before
someone mentions 'yo mama'.

'Surely this is a new thing?' you're thinking to yourself. 'It's a
result of those hip hop battles in that America.' Oh no, my friend.
Shakespeare had never heard of Eminem, but he knew that few
things sting harder than a mum cuss. In *Titus Andronicus* (it's like
the movie *Saw*, but Ancient Greekier), **Aaron** taunts his lover's sons
Demetrius and **Chiron**:

Demetrius: Villain, what hast thou done?
Aaron: That which thou canst not undo.
Chiron: Thou hast undone our mother.
Aaron: Villain, I have done thy mother.

As they said in Shakey's day, 'Verily hast he zingest thou!'

Heckler: 'Oi, ya fat git!'
Comedian: 'I'm only fat because every time I sleep with your mum she gives me a biscuit.'
Anon

Heckler: 'Why are you so fat?'
André Vincent: 'Because every time I take your mum from behind she lets me eat pizza off her back.'

Heckler to Irish comedian Andrew Ryan: 'Tarmac my drive!'
Andrew Ryan: 'I can't, I'm busy this week tarmacing your mum's drive. I know she loves getting her holes filled in.'

'Ooh, you're a big manly heckler. The last time I saw that much testosterone it was running down your mum's chin.'
Gary Delaney

Heckler: 'You're shit!'

Danielle Ward: 'If I wanted to talk to a wanker, I'd call your dad … and get him to put your mum on the phone.'

'I don't know why it is you crave this attention. What was it your uncle did to you? I know he wasn't your real uncle. He was a friend of your dad's, but golly gosh. He didn't half babysit a lot, eh? Inviting his mates from the docks round, queuing up outside your bedroom door, night after night. Is that why you think you crave the attention now? To try and get some acknowledgement as a person because for so long, so many saw you as nothing more than a warm anus to throw semen at?'

Rufus Hound

'Oh, you say that now, but tomorrow morning you will be farting my spunk … just like your mum did … but she needed the money.'

Gary Delaney

Heckler: 'Speak up, man.'

Sam Kinison: 'That's what your mom told me when I was leaving her house but I couldn't hear so well… I tried to understand her but she had my sperm gurgling in her throat, saying, "Sam, when you do the show, be sure to speak up. And tell my retarded son not to fuck with your act…" You may not recognize her when you get home – I shaved her back.'

'Why is having sex with your mom like getting involved in a knife fight? Because either way you can end up with a nasty gash on your face.'

Gary Delaney

Heckler: 'How's your momma?'

Richard Pryor: 'How's my momma? I beg your pardon. I will slap you in the mouth with my dick.'

Heckler calls out something inaudible.

George Carlin: 'Would somebody just put a dick in that guy's mouth, please? Coz that's what he wants. He's a cocksucker in disguise. He's got his mouth open because he wants someone to come in it. Now, if you wanna keep making noise, motherfucker, we can find you that way. Or are you just a punk coward asshole bullshit loud motherfucker and you're gonna shut up now so we don't find out where you're sitting? Coz if you keep it up we'll grab your ass and throw you on the fucking street where you belong with your mother. And I'm fucking her in the asshole every night anyway, so fuck you and your sister and your wife. If you've got a kid I hope your fucking kid dies in a car fire. How do you like that, you stupid cocksucker? Shut the fuck up and get the fuck out of here… [to **audience**] You know, you gotta use psychology. You've gotta be a bit of a psychologist up here and know how to appeal to a person.'

'What would your mother say if she could see you now? Or would she have too many dicks in her mouth to tell us?'
Rufus Hound

Danielle Ward (referring to **heckler**): 'That's my brother. He's thick as shit but he does make a good cup of tea. I have to bring him along.'

Heckler: 'Who ate all the pies?'
André Vincent: 'Yes, I have eaten all the pies; mainly to take the taste of your mother's twat out of my mouth.'

Jim Jefferies after putting down an abusive **male heckler**: 'I'm going to leave you alone now … like your dad did … but your grandfather never did.'

'Don't heckle. There are one hundred and forty-seven armed conflicts in the world, people killing each other left, right and centre, and if we can't get along in this little room, what chance has Israel got? Or Belfast or Baghdad? Plus it will end up in something embarrassing involving me and your mum.'
Markus Birdman

'Ssshh, for you, talking is a waste of a good mouth. If you don't mind me quoting your daddy.'
Gary Delaney

Heckled by My Children
Norman Lovett

" Any comedian who says they haven't been heckled is a liar or Steve Day (a very funny deaf comedian). I have been heckled many times and I guess I'm open to it with the style of comedy I do, which involves lots of pauses and flitting from subject to subject. People say the strangest things; I remember one woman who called out, 'I preferred you in *Red Dwarf*!' This was more an expression of preference than an insult but I still called her a bitch.

But are there any other comics, I wonder, who have been heckled by their own children?

Many years ago I did a show at the Canal Café Theatre in Little Venice, London, where I think heckling is quite rare. My wife and daughters Lily (who was then eight) and Kitty (six) came to the show and it was going well until about the halfway mark, when my daughters started heckling me. I used the old favourite comeback of asking them if they could do any better, and they said they could. I introduced them one at a time and they both performed brilliantly. Kitty did some surreal stuff about a penguin and a fly and Lily spoke about the oddness of one of her teachers. The audience loved it and so of course did I.

When she was ten, Kitty did a run at the Edinburgh Fringe and stole the show every night with her ten-minute stand-up routine. On one occasion the comedian Boothby Graffoe was in the audience and said something to Kitty and she came back with: 'Well done! You've just heckled a ten-year-old girl!' The audience collapsed with laughter. **"**

Heckler: 'What do you do for a living?'
Rodney Dangerfield: 'I get guys for your sister.'

'We've all got to put up with our disappointments; unfortunately, madam, you've got to sleep with yours.'
André Vincent

Heckler: 'Tell us a joke!'
Dan Antopolski: 'Your mum fell into some cheese sandwiches, and she got covered in cheese. Absolutely covered in it. She stank of cheese. And hundreds and hundreds of mice came from miles around, drawn to her by the smell of cheese. She was covered in mice. Overcome by them. But she was glad of the company, because YOU NEVER CALL.'

'Well, it's a night out for him … and a night off for his family.' **Jack Dee**

Where Are

You From?

Scousers are self-pitying thieves. Scots are alcoholic, tight, malnourished, tartan psychopaths. The Welsh fuck sheep. The Cornish/Norfolkian fuck their families. Yorkshiremen are proud of being from Yorkshire, and are therefore stupid because Yorkshire is rubbish. Northern Irish? You're a terrorist. Brummie? You're dull. Geordie? You sound funny and should put some bloody clothes on coz 'it's freezing oot'. Londoners are flash arseholes, too stupid to realize they're being overcharged for everything. Essex slags. Kent chavs. Mancunians are chimps in tracksuits. If you're from somewhere that sounds posh, you're basically Louis XVI. If you're from somewhere that doesn't sound posh, you're scum.

And if you're from overseas … god help you.

If the voice shouting at you from the void sounds as though it may have come from somewhere that the rest of the audience haven't – bingo. The fact that 'they're not from round here' makes them easy pickings. Bernard Manning built a career around this premise. Though, in fairness, most of the people who regularly went to see him were Mancunians, the ignorant, simian twats.

Jasper Carrott to **heckler**: 'So, where are you from?'
Heckler: 'Newark.'
Jasper Carrott: 'Is it a coincidence that you come from a place that's an anagram of wanker?'

Scottish heckler: 'Australians are so lazy they wouldn't pull a greasy stick out of a dog's arse!'
Wil Anderson: 'Mate, as a proud Australian, I don't think we give a shit. I think we're a little more concerned at what Scottish people are doing sticking it up there in the first place. How bad are you at playing fetch? What's going to happen if I pull it out, am I going to become King of England?'

Milton Jones to an **audience** he is pretending are Italian: 'You Italians, eh? What are you like?'

Heckler: 'Ciao!'

Milton Jones: 'You're like ciao? Oh I see, "goodbye". Do you have to go? What's your name?'

Heckler: 'Chow.'

Milton Jones: 'Does that get quite confusing? You phone someone and they say, "Who is it?" and you say "Chow", and they put the phone down? Yes, excellent. [To **audience**] I thought *I* was weird.'

Heckler: 'Liverpool's the spiritual home of comedy!'

Steve Williams: 'Only coz a lot of comedians go there and die!'

Heckling Your Audience
Milton Jones

 A corporate for 250 brewery staff in Bedford.

'Bit odd, this,' I quip. 'Here you are on your night off with free food and drink – surely you get that every night of the week?'

'We don't get free food and drink,' a female voice pipes up.

'Then how come you're all so fat?' says I, the comedian.

There's an audible gasp. Now I've become a callous stranger who has just insulted Margaret from Accounts; brave Margaret who has battled for years with obesity, although I only begin to realize this as she and her horizontally challenged support group walk, well, waddle, out of the room.

Afterwards, I'm surrounded.

'She's in pieces in the other room, crying!'

'Go and apologize, it's the least you can do!'

'I can only give you half your money. You only did half your time,' says the weaselly promoter. I'm not in a position to argue.

'Run to the car!' he says, as he stuffs a wodge of tenners into my hand.

'Run!? Run!?' I won't be intimidated. I walk, briskly, safe in the knowledge that they stood no chance of catching me.

Rufus Hound to a **heckler** who was shouting randomly at a gig in Austria: 'Look, man, there are only two famous Austrians – Hitler and Josef Fritzl. What was it about that list that made you think, "If I shout shit out at the comedy club tonight, maybe I can make number three!"'

Heckler (on umpteen occasions): 'Two World Wars and One World Cup!'
Henning Wehn: 'I don't remember America ever winning the World Cup.'

Heckler (on umpteen occasions): 'Two World Wars and One World Cup!'
Henning Wehn: 'Three World Cups and One World Pope!'

Heckler: 'Men up north's cocks are hard as rock; men down south's cocks are soft as fuck.'

André Vincent: 'I think you'll find that men down south just have more taste.'

Female heckler to Ian Stone (who has just finished telling an audience in Farnham a true story about being called an 'ugly big-nosed cunt'): 'Excuse me, we do not use that word in Farnham.'

Ian Stone: 'Well, what word do you use?'

Heckler: 'Front bottom.'

Ian Stone: 'Anyone who uses the word "front bottom" is definitely a cunt.'

Never Waste a Good Put-down
Arthur Smith

" Heckles come in numerous forms – one of my worst contained no words at all. I was on stage when a man stepped up from the audience and tipped the contents of a beer glass over my head. This sticky warm liquid was, it transpired, his own urine. It was so extreme I had to laugh and, well, it was a grim late-night dive in Glasgow – what did I expect?

At some venues, though, you do not anticipate heckling. One such was a laid-back early evening music event in Copenhagen. In my experience Scandinavian audiences are polite and well behaved – 'Blond, bland and blank', I used to say – but halfway through the set I was interrupted by a man in the front row putting his hand up. 'Excuse me,' he said. I was so surprised that I prepared a brutal comeback along the lines of 'Fuck off, you Danish bastard'. But the man smiled and spoke gently: 'I think you are very nice…' This is a surprisingly unsettling line for a comic. I thought, 'Why waste the put-down?' I said, 'Fuck off, you Danish bastard.'

I haven't played Denmark since… **"**

Australian heckler to **André Vincent** (following an Aussie victory in the cricket): 'Twenty-twenty, twenty-twenty!'
André Vincent: 'Listen, mate, we've got an 84-year-old man in the UK named David Attenborough who can swim with stingrays and make it back up to the surface.'

Rufus Hound: 'Do I detect an accent there? What part of Australia are you from?'
Heckler: 'Actually, I'm from New Zealand.'
Rufus Hound: 'Awww. How sweet. He's pretending there's a difference.'*

*This works equally well with Canadians – although you have to ask them what part of America they're from, as asking them which bit of Australia they're from really confuses everyone.

Milton Jones: 'So, where do you live?'

Heckler replies.

Milton Jones: 'OK. Why do you live?'

Henning Wehn to an **Irish heckler**: 'When they refer to "the Troubles" – do they mean you?'

Heckler (after hearing Brendon Burns make a stream of jokes about Liverpool): 'Liverpool is amazing!'

Brendon Burns: '"Liverpool is amazing."

If your yardstick of amazing is fucking Liverpool, do you also get excited at night when it goes dark? … You fucking hobbit. You moron. You spastic. Kill yourself. That's terrible. "Liverpool is amazing!" And so are chips. You know what else is amazing? Brown sauce on a bit of bacon. How about you go down to the Costa del Sol where you were conceived on the back dash of a Ford Escort. You fucking lolly-yanking retard. You fuckwit. I'm destroying you in front of a room full of people. Is tonight the night you're gonna kill yourself? How's it gonna happen? Is it gonna be by rope? Will you stick your head in an oven? … That's what happens, son … you heckle, you get shot down, you fucking foetus. Climb back in the bucket, you abortion. Can six guys just pick him up and remove him from the room please… By the way, tell your mum she still owes my dog fuck-money. Pinhead. Watch that head roll as people kick it into a gutter and then block the gutter with your own shit. You're so fucking empty, when you shit there's no enzymes in you to fucking digest food, you just consume pineapple and pineapple comes out… You long-lost son of Wayne Rooney. You illegitimate Wayne Rooney spunkard. Wayne Rooney fucking jacked off into a cup, it fell into a puddle and nine months later you popped out.'

I Don't Come to 8
Your Workplace

So far, the put-downs in this book are targeted at things over which the heckler has no control: appearance, parentage, intelligence, where they grew up, etc. However, the comedian who wishes to conquer their challenger in a more superior fashion may decide that these Achillean heels are simply not spiteful enough.

Instead, they'll damn their assailant for the choices they have made, thus striking them in their very soul. No more immediate indicator of their life's quality exists than what they do for a living. If you're being a dick in a comedy club and let slip that you are an estate agent/traffic warden/banker, your life is about to be made as intolerable as you make others'.

But, you are no doubt thinking, 'What if what they do is good?' Fair point, but clearly you have none of the venom required to make it as a leather-hided circuit comedian. If cultural relativism has taught us anything, it's that nothing is good. You could be a volunteer, building schools in rural India for orphans, but you know what I'm thinking?

1. I'm not surprised you volunteer. No one would pay a twat like you.
2. Rural India, eh? You mean you had to travel halfway around the world to realize that the only people who are happy to see you can't understand a word you're saying?
3. Why is it you're wont to hang out with orphaned kids so much? What's your plan, Mr Glitter?

Meryl O'Rourke to a crowd of **heckling plumbers**: 'Can you shut the fuck up now? I know as plumbers this concept will be alien to you, but when I'm employed to do an evening's work I like to actually provide the service I've been paid for.'

'I don't come to your workplace and tell you how to sweep up/flip burgers/knock the sailors' cocks out of your mouth.'

Anon

Jim Smallman to **heckler**: 'What do you do for a living?'
Heckler: 'I work in a tampon factory. Make a joke out of that.'
Jim Smallman: 'I won't make a joke out of that, but I do have a question: would you say that the run-up to Christmas is your busiest period?'

Drunken squaddie at a military gig: 'You're a comedian, do your job and tell some jokes.'
Steve Williams: 'You're a soldier, do your job, follow orders and shut up!'

Rufus Hound to a guy who started shouting at him from an office party: 'Wow! So I met Sharon in Accounts, Lisa from HR and a couple of dudes from Marketing. Let me guess … you're the office cunt.'*

*This got an enormous cheer from everyone from that office, so I guess I was right.

'Ignore this guy. They don't get much shore leave on the HMS *Cockend*.'
Brendan Dodds

Memories of the Tunnel Palladium

Jim Tavaré

❝ My recollections of performing at the notorious Tunnel Palladium in Greenwich, run by the late Malcom Hardee, still give me nightmares. I used to open with the line 'Good evening, I'm a schizophrenic', to which a heckler once responded, 'Why don't you both fuck off?' My act included impressions from the Starship *Enterprise*. During my routine I heard, 'It's comedy, Jim, but not as we know it'.

Later I discovered a niche performing with my double bass, provoking heckles such as 'It's a midget with a violin!' and 'It doesn't matter if he dies on stage, he's brought his own coffin.' I used to do a sound effect on my bass of a man sawing off his wooden leg. At this point someone in the front row once took off his prosthetic leg and plonked it on the stage.

I would appear every Sunday and I was so entertainingly bad that Malcolm created a segment called 'Get Jim Tavaré Off In Under Two Minutes'. Dressed in white tie and tails, I was fair game for the taunters and found my most effective weapon was simply: 'Shut up, ya cunt!' (I would only use this when absolutely necessary, like a superhero uses his special powers.)

Malcolm had his own special methods of dealing with hecklers. On one occasion a group of rowdy drunks chose to sit at the front. It was a long night and one of them fell asleep. At the end of the show Malcolm unzipped his trousers and urinated in the guy's mouth. The heckler remained asleep during all of this, then woke up wondering why the entire audience was laughing at him. ❞

'Nice to see the Bishop of Durham enjoying himself…'
Arthur Smith

Ian Stone: 'What do you do, sir?'
Man in audience: 'I'm an engineer.'
Ian Stone: 'What type of engineer?'
Man: 'You wouldn't understand.'
Ian Stone: 'Try me.'
Man: 'Supersonic gas solution.'
Ian Stone [quick as a flash]: 'Expialidocious!'

Rufus Hound to a **heckler** who it transpires is unemployed: 'So is that why you're shouting bullshit at me? Listen, I reckon, if you work really hard, get a decent CV together and perfect your interview technique, this time next year you could be collecting the trolleys at Lidl. Or at least blowing the guy that collects the trolleys at Lidl for loose change.'

Acknowledgements

Huge thanks are due to all the comics who provided put-downs and stories for this book. It would not have been possible without you.

We are also indebted to the following for supplying photographs:

Avalon: pages 22, 42, 76
Charles Bradshaw: page 103
Ray Burmiston: page 60
Nick Farrington-Smith: page 19
Justin Griffiths-Williams: page 39
Sally Grosart: page 25
© Andy Hollingworth Archive: pages 14, 29, 41, 45, 56, 72, 75, 79, 80, 85, 105, 106, 111, 119
Garry Hunter: page 66
Edward Moore: pages 4, 31, 46, 71, 93, 94, 121
Ellis O'Brien: page 51
Chris Potter: page 115
Studio 1B Photography: page 63
Laura Tavaré: page 124
Ian West/PA Archive: page 34

The following people provided invaluable help with permissions requests, contact details and other things: Debi Allen, Richard Allen-Turner, Rob Aslett, Alex Beedell, Sally Carter, Lucy Chaloner, Sophie Chapman, Debra Clavey, Carla Clee, Vivienne Clore, Kim Graham, Rick Hughes, Joss Jones, Sarah King, Robert Kirby, Charlotte Knee, Christian Knowles, Warren Lakin, Nathalie Laurent-Marke, David Lazenby, Corrie McGuire, Kerry McIntosh, Charlene McManus, Mark Makin, Lauren Marks, Lee Martin, Simon Mason, Katherine Minnis, Martin Mullaney, Lynn Nakama, Maureen O'Connor, Debbie Pisani, Tom Searle, Susie Skinner, Charlotte Smith, Vivienne Smith, James Taylor, Lisa Thomas, Brett Vincent, Lisa White, Hannah Wilkinson and Ian Wilson. Hugs and kisses to all of you, and apologies to anyone who has been accidentally left out.

Observant readers will have noticed that Nigel Planer's put-down as Neil from *The Young Ones* on page 67 contains a line about sausages that is remarkably similar to Arnold Brown's one on page 35 about potatoes. We just wanted to point out here that Arnold originated the joke and agreed that Nigel could adapt it for his act.

Every effort has been made to obtain the necessary permissions with reference to copyright material, both illustrative and quoted. We apologize for any omissions in this respect and will be pleased to make the appropriate acknowledgements in any future edition.

RUFUS HOUND

BEING RUDE

Live at THE 100 CLUB

18

18

DVD VIDEO

OUT NOW ON DVD!

COMEDY CENTRAL